TOO GOOD TO BE TRUE

Lifetime Tax-Free Retirement Income

INDEXED UNIVERSAL LIFE

DISCLAIMER

The material contained inside this book is for educational and informational purposes only. No responsibility can be taken for any results or outcomes resulting from the use of this material.

While the author has made every attempt to provide information that is both accurate and effective, the author does not assume any responsibility for the accuracy or use/misuse of this information.

All the information and facts were correct and up to date at the time of writing.

DEDICATION:

This book is dedicated to all the families across the nation in need of protecting their loved ones and securing their financial futures. I hope this book will bring some clarity to those searching for solutions.

And to my son Konnor Jr., in which I am so proud and lucky to watch grow into an incredible human being. You are my heartbeat.

CONTENTS

INTRODUCTION

With the rising costs of living such as housing, gas, and even the price of milk, what are you doing to beat inflation - or at least keep up with it? Many Americans haven't the slightest clue on which investments are worthy of putting their hard-earned dollars into. Seeking guidance, many will turn to stock brokers or financial planners. But those two options not only cost a fortune in fees, it also puts their savings at risk without any guarantees of profits in return.

Stock brokers will charge you for every single trade they make on your behalf - no matter if the advice given turns out to be right or wrong. If you end up losing money on that stock, you paid the broker commissions for that trade. Financial Planners can charge hundreds of dollars per hour to advise you on your portfolio of investments. Again, even if the advised investments lost money later, you already paid the invoice for their consulting.

However, there is one class of financial services professional who can guarantee stock market-like gains with absolutely ZERO chance of losses. And that would be your Life Insurance Agent!

Unlike other financial industry professionals, you would never pay an Insurance Agent for a consult or any commissions for the purchase of a policy. Because they get paid directly from the insurance carriers they represent.

You're probably wondering how a Life Insurance Agent can make such amazing investment guarantees. Especially when other industry professionals can't. The answer is quite simple.

The financial instrument which guarantees (in writing) stock market-like gains without ever suffering any of the market losses, is a life insurance product!

Think about that for a second...

When the stock market is up, you profit. But when the stock market is down, your account holds still and never loses a single a penny!

...sound too good to be true? Keep reading.

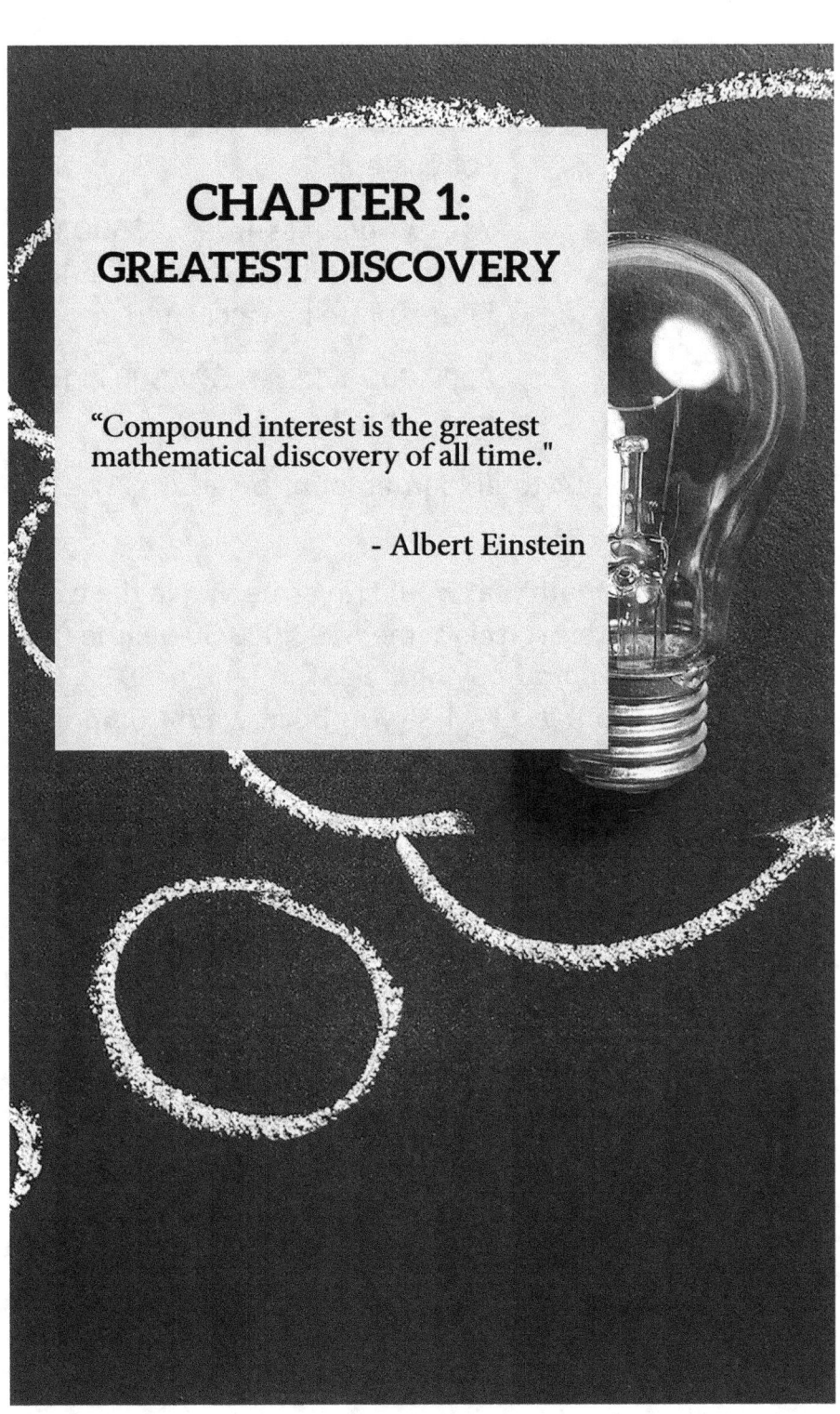

CHAPTER 1:
GREATEST DISCOVERY

"Compound interest is the greatest
mathematical discovery of all time."

- Albert Einstein

Typically, 1 + 1 = 2. But in the world of finance, 1 + 1 can sometimes equal 10. That's due to compound interest.

For example:

You would assume a $500,000 30-year mortgage loan at a 4.5% interest rate be calculated as:

$500,000 x 4.5% = $22,500 in total interest to be paid.

Thus, bringing your total loan amount owed to $522,500 payable over 30 years.

If it were simple math that would ring true. But in the world of compound interest, this same $500,000 30-year loan at 4.5% would have you paying back the lender $912,300! That's nearly double of what you borrowed. Compound interest turns that 4.5% into an interest rate of nearly 82%!

Understand that time equals money. Sending in a payment resets the compounding clock. The longer you take to make a payment, the more interest is accruing. When at all possible, try to make payments quicker to save on interest.

Utilizing this same principle, you can pay your mortgage off nearly 5 years faster by sending in bi-weekly payments to your lender. It doesn't cost you a penny extra to do it either. So instead of sending in your regular full mortgage payment of $2,500 once a month, you'd simply send in a

half payment of $1,250 every two weeks. In this scenario, you'd be eliminating 4.5 years (54 months) of mortgage payments. $2,500 x 54 months = $71,000 in savings! Send in an extra mortgage payment each year and you can reduce the time and total costs of the loan exponentially.

Compound Interest is a 2-way street. You can pay compounding interest, or you can earn it! You work hard for your money. In return, make sure it's working hard for you!

Compound Interest is what every investor should fully comprehend. It is the understanding of how to double your money, and the amount of time it takes to do so.

Rule of 72

The 'Rule of 72' is a straightforward way of determining how long an investment takes to double your money. Here's how it works:

Divide 72 by the number of years to get the interest rate

you'd need to earn for your money to double during that time. For instance, if you wanted to double your investment in 8 years, you'd simply divide 72 by 8!

72 ÷ 8 (years) = 9%

You would need to earn an interest rate of 9% in order for your money to double in 8 years.

Conversely, to calculate the amount of time it would take for your account to deplete due to inflation: Divide 72 by the inflation rate. For example, at an inflation rate of 3.25%, divide 72 by 3.25 and the answer is 22 years to reduce the total amount of your money.

There are many investment products that offer higher yields than the current rate of inflation. Many such products also come with risks of potentially losing your entire investment.

Not to worry, we'll soon cover the product that guarantees you zero losses – ever.

CHAPTER 2:
TAX HISTORY

In 1913, when the current federal income tax program was introduced, your effective federal income tax rate would have been just 1.0%. After the Great Depression Era of the 1930's, to help the economic recovery, tax rates spiked to 90% for some! Yes, you read that correctly.

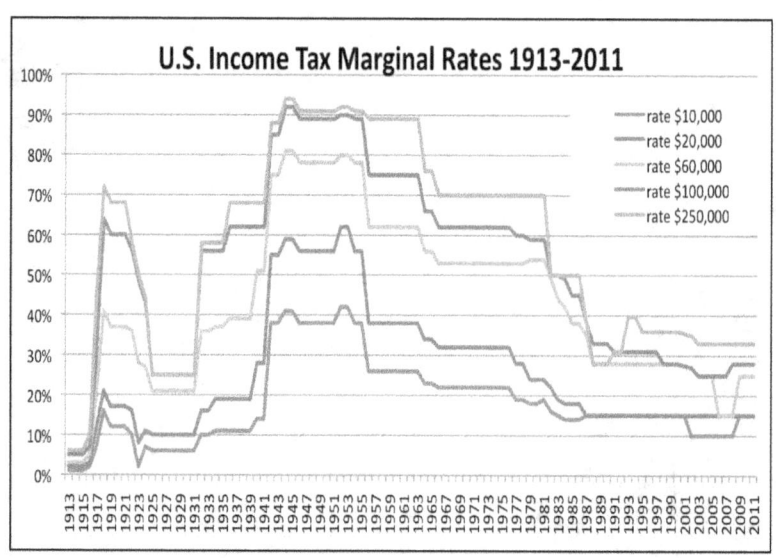

U.S. Income Tax Marginal Rates 1913-2011

- rate $10,000
- rate $20,000
- rate $60,000
- rate $100,000
- rate $250,000

Today, we're in a system of graduated income taxes. Meaning every US citizen's first $8,700 is taxed 10%, the next $26,649 is taxed 15%, and so on, all the way up to $388,350, at which point, every additional dollar that's earned is taxed at 35%.

The reality is, based on historical data, we've been experiencing some of the lowest income tax rates in history since The Great Depression Era. But with the government being trillions of dollars in debt, and Social Security nearing bankruptcy, one cannot

reasonably expect income tax rates to remain the same forever.

If you believe that income tax rates will increase sometime in the future, then you should really do something about it - today. ..Before it's too late.

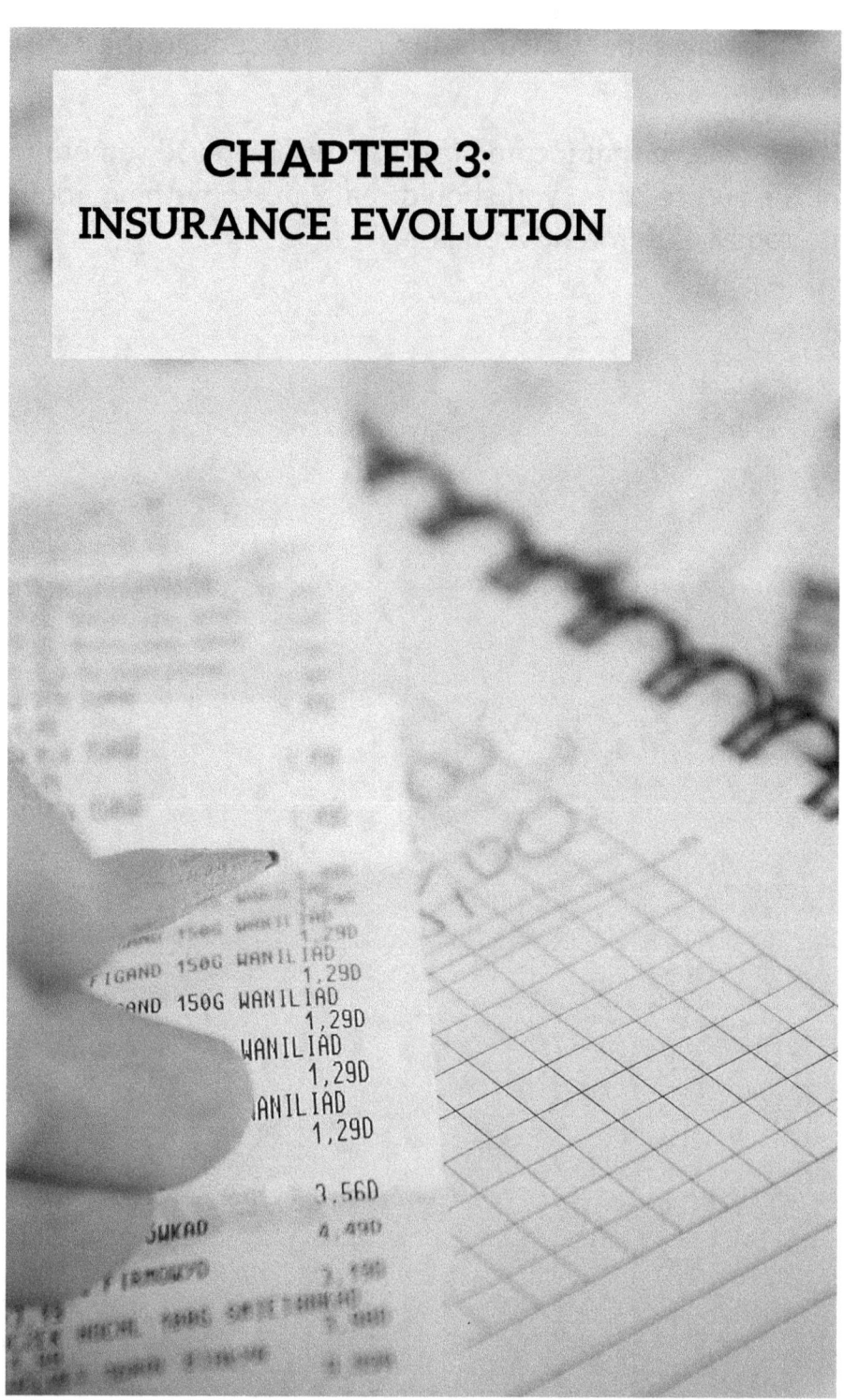

CHAPTER 3:
INSURANCE EVOLUTION

ife insurance in the United States can be traced all the way back to the 1700's. Today, the US is the world's largest insurance market in premium volume. Over $1.2 Trillion of gross premiums were written in 2013 alone. Life insurance policies have evolved quite a bit in the past few hundred years.

Here's a quick look at the evolution of some products:

Term Life policies are temporary life insurance policies, meaning they have an expiration date. Therefore, these policies do not build any cash value. They can be for terms of 5 years, all the way up to 30 years. Term Life policies rarely ever pay out for one of two reasons:

1. People stop paying their monthly premiums allowing the policy to lapse.

2. They reached the end of the policy term and are still alive.

Either way, paying into something for many years and not receiving any monetary benefit in the end can be quite disheartening. When customers become dissatisfied with a product, they stop buying it. Insurance carriers' lifeblood is the monthly premiums that they collect. And since customers were wanting more from their policies, the product offerings needed to improve.

*Mortgage Protection Insurance is usually an affordable Decreasing Term Life insurance policy that amortizes at the same rate of your mortgage. It guarantees a tax-free death benefit to your beneficiaries in the event of your death. These funds can be used to help pay off the mortgage.

Whole Life policies were the answer to those looking for

more than just Term Life. This option would be permanent for one's "whole" life. This policy never expires AND builds cash value over time. The excess of monthly premiums over and above the cost of insurance is credited to the Cash Value account of the policy where it earns interest. One could borrow against or withdraw funds when needed. Although this was a greater option to the Term Life policy, consumers eventually needed even more from their policies.

* Final Expense life insurance is a Whole Life policy designed with the purpose of helping surviving family members pay for their loved ones' funeral expenses. They are usually marketed to senior citizens. The application process is relatively easy with most carriers not requiring a medical exam. Death benefits are usually between $5,000-$50,000. In California, the costs of a funeral can range between $7,000 to more than $20,000 depending on chosen services, casket, plot, and headstone.

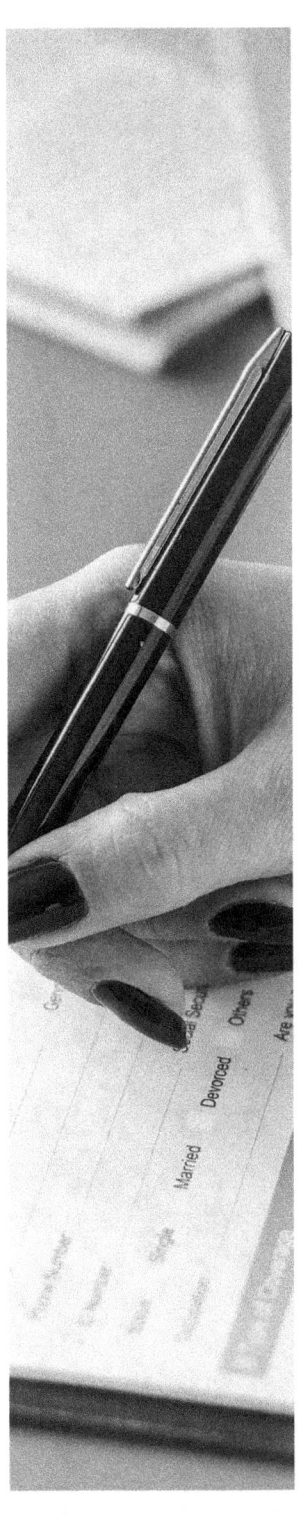

Having a permanent life insurance policy came with the same burden as with Term Life policies, which meant that the interval premiums needed to be paid in full – or risk cancellation of the policy.

Universal Life (UL) policies were the answer that many Americans desperately needed. It is a whole life policy with the added benefit of flexible monthly premiums. With flexible premium options, one could for example, pay only the "minimum payment" which is usually half of the regular monthly premium, and the policy would still stay in force. This option comes in handy when life throws a curveball; whether it be a job loss, or the holidays, or a self-employed individual with irregular monthly income.

Note: Making just the minimum monthly payment would impact the growth of the Cash Value account.

But with an industry that requires the constant flow of incoming monthly premiums, the carriers were forced to do even more. The result meant that the product would once again evolve. Except this time, the product transformation was designed to be the last policy that any individual would ever need.

Introducing the Indexed Universal Life (IUL). Just like the Universal Life policy, the Indexed Universal Life (IUL) is also a permanent policy that builds cash value and allows for flexible premium payment options.

But IUL's are unique for 3 additional reasons:

- Indexing which allows your cash account to earn stock market-like gains, without suffering from any of the market losses.

- Living Benefits Riders (LB's) with a qualifying Chronic, Critical, or Terminal Illness (such as a stroke, cancer, or heart attack), the policy would pay out a portion of the death benefit in advance – while the insured is still alive!

- Lifetime Income Rider when structured properly, the insured cannot outlive this income. Meaning it will pay you income for the rest of your life – tax free.

Indexed Universal Life policies cover you for all of life's needs, whether you:
- Die too soon
  (Death Benefit)

- Get sick along the way,
  (Living Benefits)

- Live too long
  (Lifetime Income)

CHAPTER 4:
INDEXING

The market meltdown of 2008 caused many Americans to lose tens of thousands of dollars from their 401(k) accounts. What took individuals so many years to accumulate, was lost in the blink of an eye. People were stunned as they were not aware their "retirement accounts" were exposed to any risk. When the average person deposits contributions into their retirement account, they're expecting that money to be there at retirement - plus interest.

Indexing guarantees exactly that - you will never lose a single penny from your account. While participating in the stock market upside and receiving gains, you are fully protected from any downside. Never suffering any of the market losses. Many individuals will purchase an IUL for this reason alone. With the added benefits of life insurance being secondary. Whatever your main concerns and goals may be, having an IUL provides great diversification to any portfolio of a sound retirement plan.

Every insurance carrier has 2 accounts: A Separate Account and a General Account. The Separate Account is where funds are used to make investments. Your money is never at risk and safe by being in the General Account.

IULs have a (ceiling) cap rate and a floor rate. The cap rate is usually 9% - 14%. With a floor rate typically of 0%. Most carriers that offer IULs today will use the S&P 500 stock market index to mirror. So let's look at some scenarios:

You have an IUL with a 12% cap and 0% floor.

If the S&P 500 goes up 22% in any given year, your account will be credited the max cap rate of 12%. If the S&P 500 is down 8% for the year and the rest of the country is losing money, your account will not go lower than the 0% floor. So no gains in that down year, but zero losses either.

Policy illustrations will use a 30-year lookback period on the S&P 500. With an IUL offering a 12% cap and 0% floor, your account would average nearly 7% in annual gains! Compounding interest for you year after year. Tax-free!

TOO GOOD TO BE TRUE

CHAPTER 5:
QUALIFIED vs. NON-QUALIFIED

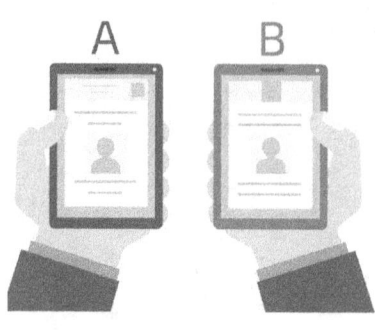

A   B

When investing, you have two tax plan options: Qualified or Non-Qualified.

Qualified plans are offered by companies to their employees. In Qualified investment plans such as 401(k)s, IRAs, and some profit-sharing plans, contributions are made via payroll deduction. Taxes are not deducted at the point of deposit. But instead, are taken in later years during the period of withdrawals. This allows for more money to be initially deposited into the plan allowing for faster accumulation – which sounds good in theory. But keep in mind, at some point taxes will have to be paid on all that money.

In a Non-Qualified plan (such as an IUL), the money you deposit into it would be with after-tax dollars. By choosing this non-qualified plan, you're investing with money that you've already paid taxes on, thus alleviating any future tax burden on that money.

Which would you rather?

Qualified scenario: $100 is deducted from your paycheck to invest in your 401(k). (because taxes were never collected, the IRS basically becomes your investment partner) The account grows to $1 Million. At retirement, you now pay taxes on the entire $1 Million dollars (approximately $350,000 in today's tax rate).

Non-Qualified scenario: $100 is deducted from your bank account and put into an IUL (Non-Qualified plan). You've already paid taxes on the $100, so you're now free to do with it whatever you wish. Your IUL cash account grows to $1 Million. (the IRS doesn't care because they've already collected their share). At retirement, you owe zero on the entire $1 Million dollars. (That's ZERO)

These two scenarios are also true upon one's death. If you have $1 Million dollars in your 401k and believe your family would get $1 Million upon your death, think again. Nearly half is gone to taxes. Yet, if you past away with an IUL worth $1 Million, that entire amount is paid to your beneficiaries.

 You should always consult with your 401k administrator and/or tax professional with questions. When thinking about your retirement dollars, it may be a smarter choice to pay taxes at today's low rate, rather than the expected increased rate of tomorrow.

CHAPTER 6:
LIFE INSURANCE
SAVINGS ACCOUNT

An IUL has an "Accumulation Value Account" and a "Cash Value Account". The Accumulation Account is the amount you have that's earning you interest. Whereas the Cash Value Account also known as the Cash Surrender Account, is the amount of cash you have available to you at any time. But for ease of conversation and explanation, let's consider the combination of these accounts in your policy to be your "Life Insurance Savings Account".

The average rate of return on an IUL with a 12% cap is approximately 7%. That's a great return when your money is compounding for you tax free. That's also nearly 30 times more interest than what some banks are currently paying: at a quarter of one percent (0.25%). You would even have to pay taxes on that earned interest from the bank!

IUL benefits can be structured at Level or Increasing terms. When structured at level, any cash loans or withdrawals from the policy will decrease the death benefit. But when structured with the increasing option, the Life Insurance Savings Account grows in addition to the death benefit! For example, if you had a $500,000 IUL policy set at increasing benefit. And 10 years later had $100,000 in your cash account when you passed away, your beneficiary would receive the $500,000 death benefit PLUS the $100,000 that was available in your Life Insurance Savings Account!

And here's one of the most exciting features of the Life Insurance Savings Account when compared to an ordinary bank account:

Scenario A) You have a regular bank savings account with $100,000 in it earning you interest. You withdraw $50,000. You now have a remaining balance of only $50,000 that is earning you interest. $100,000 - $50,000 = $50,000.

Scenario B) You have a Life Insurance Savings Account from an IUL with $100,000 in it earning you interest. You withdraw $50,000. Although your remaining "available balance" is now only $50,000, you STILL have the total of $100,000 earning you interest! Because that money was withdrawn as a loan. So your "accumulation value account" which is earning you interest never decreases!

$100,000 - $50,000 = $100,000!
Which sounds better to you?

People use bank accounts to pay their bills – but what everyone should have is a Life Insurance Savings Account to pay themselves.

CHAPTER 7:
DEATH BENEFIT

Life insurance benefits are paid once the insured individual has deceased. Beneficiaries would then file a claim with the insurance company to receive the death benefit. Most claims are paid within 60 days. The following are just a few of the payout options that can be chosen;

LUMP SUM — As the name implies, the entire death benefit amount is received in one single payment.

LIFE INCOME — This option enables the beneficiary to receive a fixed, monthly payment for the reminder of their life. The payment amount will be determined by the person's age and gender.

LIFE INCOME (PERIOD CERTAIN) — In this option, a portion of the payout is guaranteed annually for a certain period of time. The longer the period, the lower the annual payment will be.

INTEREST INCOME — In this option, a portion of the death benefit is put aside to earn interest which is then paid out to the person on a monthly or annual basis.

SPECIFIC INCOME — In this option, the person can choose how much money they want to receive and on what basis until the death benefit has been fully paid out.

*Death Benefits are paid out tax free up to the original benefit amount. If certain payout options chosen accrues interest, you may be subject to taxes on the interest earnings. Always consult with a tax professional with tax questions.

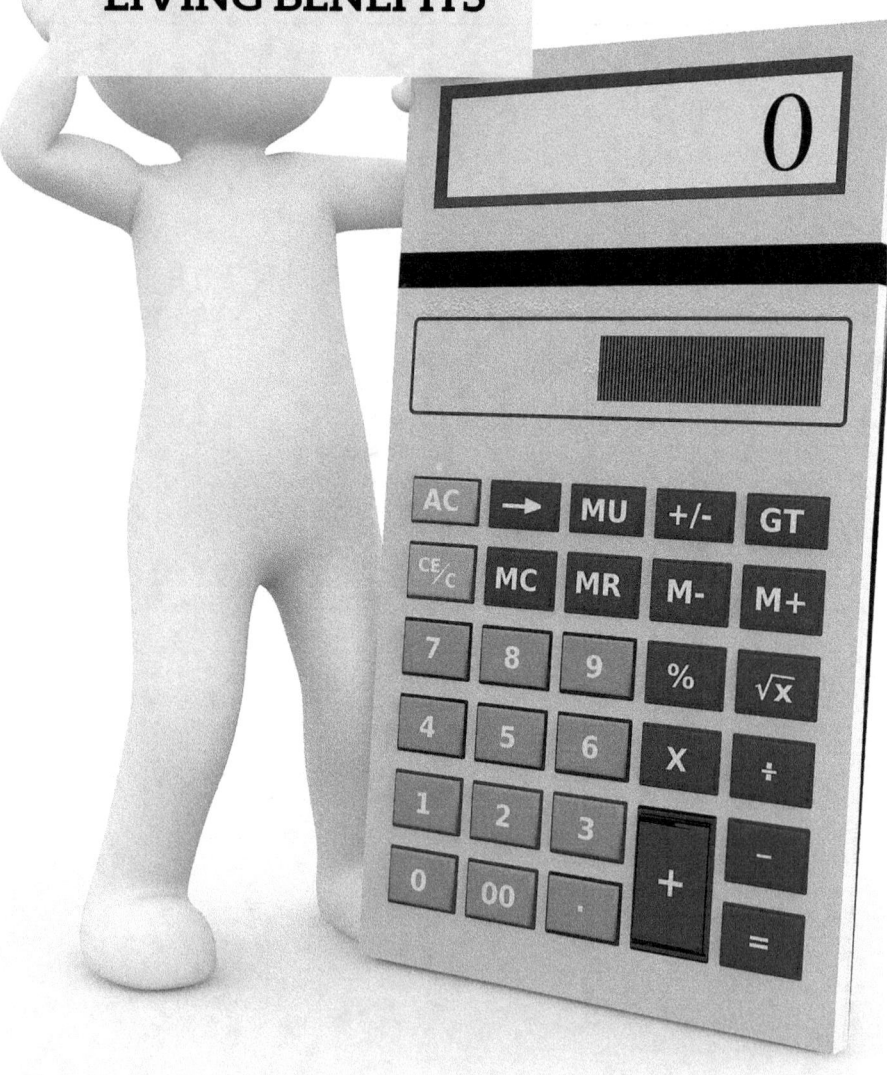

CHAPTER 8:
LIVING BENEFITS

Not all IULs offer Living Benefits (LBs). Typically, the ones that don't offer Living Benefits offer a higher interest cap rate; example 16% versus the typical 9-14%. Those looking for a more aggressive return on investment may opt to go with the higher interest product instead of getting the one that includes Living Benefits. But one should be cautious foregoing Living Benefits because a catastrophic health disaster can strike anyone at any time.

Nearly 700,000 Americans file bankruptcy every year due to enormous debt from medical bills. And of those individuals that filed bankruptcy, 75% of them had health insurance!

Living Benefits allow the policy owner to access cash from their life insurance policy while they are still living, in the event of a qualifying illness such as:

Terminal Illness - When diagnosed with a terminal illness such as cancer, in which the person is expected to die within 24 months (in most states).

Chronic Illness - A qualifying Chronic Illness means that the insured is unable to perform any 2 of the 6 Activities of Daily Living (ADL). Which are: eating, bathing, dressing, toileting, transference, and continence.

Critical Illness - When diagnosed with a serious illness, such as a stroke or heart attack.

Critical Injury – Some carriers now offer this coverage in the event of paralysis.

*Note that any Living Benefit payout would deduct from the Death Benefit value.

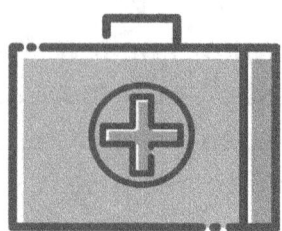

For example:

- $500,000 life insurance policy

- $75,000 living benefits paid out due to a qualifying event
_____

= $425,000 remaining death benefit to be paid out to beneficiary in the future

LIVING BENEFITS VS. SUPPLEMENTAL INSURANCE

 Some companies offer what are known as Supplemental Insurance which are standalone policies. They are relatively inexpensive and nearly everyone gets approved. They are the same type coverages as the Living Benefits we've discussed that are in a life insurance policy. But there are major differences in terms of costs, qualifications, and benefit amounts. Here are some examples of what these supplemental insurance coverages look like:

- **Terminal Illness Supplemental Insurance** – You select the amount of desired coverage based on your budget and needs. It usually pays between $25,000 - $50,000 if you ever get diagnosed with cancer. Costs range between $80-$120 a month depending on age and gender.

- **Critical Illness Supplemental Insurance** – Again, you select the amount of coverage based on needs. Costs are approximately $80-$100 a month.

- **Chronic Illness Supplemental Insurance** – This coverage will pay up to $1,000 a month for a maximum of 12 months. Costs are approximately $80-$100 a month. (if you were unable to work due to a chronic illness, would $1,000 a month be enough to pay your monthly bills and cover costs of living?) ..probably not.

As you can see in this example, this individual would be spending approximately $240 a month for all three supplemental insurance coverages - with very low benefit amounts. ..Having some coverage is always better than no coverage at all.

But let's say this individual took that same $240 a month and instead purchased an Indexed Universal Life policy that included Living Benefits. They would get all 3 Illness Riders AND a death benefit AND tax-free income at retirement! And let's assume this person would be able to purchase a $250,000 policy with that $240 monthly premium.

If they were to have a Chronic Illness, the IUL will pay out up to 2% of the face amount.

$250,000 x 2% = $5,000 a month!

Compare that to only $1,000 the standalone supplemental insurance policy provides. As you can see, Living Benefits within an IUL policy can provide much more in benefits than the supplemental insurance. And best of all, Living Benefits within an IUL are simply included!

CHAPTER 9:
LIFETIME
TAX-FREE INCOME

To qualify for the Lifetime Income Rider benefit, most carriers require insureds to pay premiums for a minimum of 10 years and be at least age 60 to begin receiving income. Once this rider is activated, the insured no longer pays any monthly premiums. Instead, the policy would begin paying the insured an income at intervals selected (monthly or annually). This rider will pay an insured to the maximum age of 120 years old. In other words, when structured properly the insured cannot outlive this income. It will pay steady income for the rest of the insured's life – tax free.

Here are a few hypothetical examples of IULs at work:

MALE

Age 22

$500 monthly premium

Beginning at Age 65:

$1,098,515 cash available in Life Insurance Savings Account

$89,169 tax-free annual income. For life!

$500 a month today = $7,400 a month at retirement.

That's nearly a 15x return on investment!

FEMALE

Age 25

$500 monthly premium

Beginning at Age 65:

$910,783 cash available in Life Insurance Savings Account

$77,070 tax-free annual income.

$500 a month today = $6,400 a month at retirement.

That's a 13x return on investment!

FEMALE

Age 40

$500 monthly premium

Beginning at Age 65:

$272,665 cash available in Life Insurance Savings Account

$26,764 tax-free annual income.

$500 a month today = $2,200 a month at retirement.

That's over 4x return on investment!

Amazing cash available and tax-free retirement income. Plus all the insurance coverage!

Curious of what your numbers would look like?

CHAPTER 10:
401(K) VS. IUL

M any individuals with 401(k)s are unaware their withdrawals at retirement will incur income tax. And if they withdraw 401(k) funds before age 59 ½, they will incur a 10% tax penalty in addition to their regular income tax rate. Individuals with IULs can pull money out of their policies without owing any taxes.

401(k) owners who need cash may request and apply for a loan from their 401(k) administrators. And IF approved, 401(k) owners must make installment payments for repayment of that loan - plus interest! This paid interest is not credited to their account. IUL owners who need money from their policy need not apply for it. They simply request the desired amount from the available cash balance, and it's wired to their account within days. These loans need not ever by repaid by the insured. If they pass away with an outstanding loan balance, it is simply deducted from the policy's death benefit amount.

The average 401(k) will run out of funds just 7-8 years into retirement! Do the math: A person makes $50,000 a year in income. They retire with $250,000 in their 401(k). Without drastically altering their current standard of living, they would need approximately $50,000 a year to continue their lifestyle. So withdrawing $50,000 a year from that $250,000 401(k) account would deplete their retirement savings just a few years into retirement. An IUL offers Lifetime Tax Free Income at retirement that never runs out.

Let's not forget about what happened to the 401(k) accounts across the nation when the market crashed not long ago. Millions of Americans lost their retirement savings. With the collective losses amounting to nearly $2.4 Trillion! With an Indexed Universal Life policy, you are guaranteed to never suffer any losses – ever.

TOO GOOD TO BE TRUE

You might be saying to yourself, this sounds "too good to be true!" And unfortunately for many people, it sadly is. Because IULs offer such an extensive and robust amount of coverage, insurance carriers must hedge their bets by only approving the applications of healthy individuals. If you have any concerns about your previous medical history, consult with an IUL Life Insurance Agent before applying. They will be able to go over the underwriting guidelines with you.

So now that you know the basic mechanics of an IUL, you may be very curious as to what your specific numbers may be. Be sure to only contact an experienced Life Insurance Agent with knowledge of Indexed Universal Life policies to run your specific policy illustration. An experienced agent will listen to your goals and tailor the policy to your needs.

* IUL application process may take anywhere from 1 week to 2 months for underwriting approval.

* Depending on the applicant, carriers may or may not require fluids or additional information.

Whether your concern was to protect your family's financial future, coverage for a possible major medical event, or retirement needs - the IUL has you covered.

Finally, one policy that truly does it all:

- Tax-free death benefit to your loved ones in the event of dying too soon.

- Living Benefits to cover you if you get sick along the way.

- Tax-free retirement income – for the rest of your life.

- Indexed to protect your money, with a generous cap rate to grow it.

You may be pinching yourself, thinking "this IUL couldn't possibly get any better".

Well it can. ..and it has!

You can now get an Indexed Universal Life policy with a NO CAP rate option!!

So if the stock market goes up 35%, your account gains 35%!! (minus the spread)

For a quick personalized illustration, speak with an IUL specialist today!

www.ingramcontent.com/pod-product-compliance
Lightning Source LLC
Chambersburg PA
CBHW071115220526
45467CB00004B/1901